JED PASCOE'S

THE FUNNY SIDE OF 30s

Published in the UK by
POWERFRESH Limited
3 Gray Street
Northampton
NN1 3QQ

Telephone 44 01604 30996
Facsimile 44 01604 21013

Cover and interior illustration Jed Pascoe

Cover and interior layout Powerfresh

THE FUNNY SIDE OF 30S
ISBN 1 874125 26 0

Printed in the UK by Avalon Print Northampton
      Powerfresh October 1995

WHEN TRYING TO
SPOT AN OVER-30,
LOOK FOR THE
FOLLOWING
CERT GIVEAWAYS:

① SIDEWAYS-PRESSED
FLARES AND
GLITTER PLATFORM
BOOTS

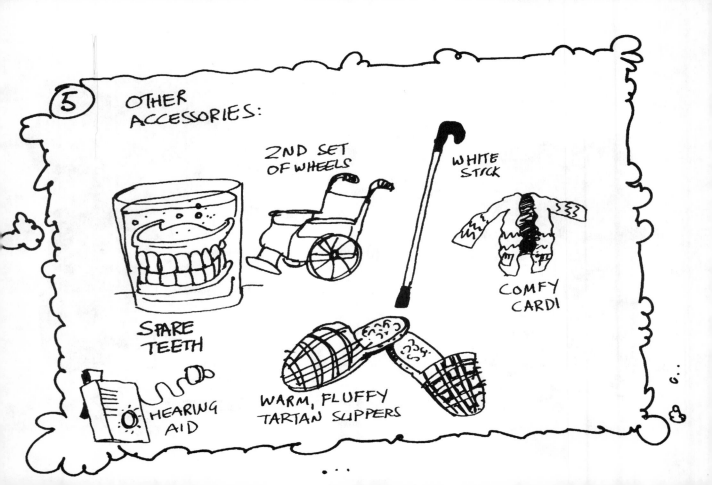

EMILY WOULD GO TO QUITE EXTRAORDINARY LENGTHS TO PREVENT A DOUBLE CHIN....

ONCE AGAIN, THE PRESENCE OF HIS CHILDHOOD PET
GAVE AWAY ROGER'S TRUE AGE...

KATHERINE HAD TO BE SURGICALLY REMOVED FROM
HER SPORTS CAR IN FAVOUR OF A FAMILY ESTATE...

THE BATHROOM MIRROR TOLD NO LIES.
SARAH TRULY LOOKED HER AGE THIS MORNING..

RICHARD'S ATTEMPT TO KEEP ABREAST OF CONTEMPORARY HAIR STYLES FELL CATASTROPHICALLY SHORT OF THE MARK

JED PASCOE
NATIONAL AND INTERNATIONAL
AWARD WINNING
CARTOONIST.
LIVING PROOF THAT
EMPTY VESSELS MAKE
MOST NOISE..
TOTALLY CONFUSED BY
LIFE, HE LIVES MAINLY
IN HIS BELEAGURED
IMAGINATION — WHICH
IS ENOUGH TO
CONFUSE ANYONE. AND
STILL LOOKING FOR FAME
AND FORTUNE, IF ANYONE
OUT THERE IS INTERESTED.